AF374794

FROM SILENT TO

Spoken

Poems by Anika Yadav

This is the story of how a girl breaks her silence,

from quiet to whispers, and finally speech.

A blend of free verse, with a couple of haikus sprinkled in–

short and sweet, like chocolate chips in a warm cookie.

From quirky robots to quietly sweeping,

a silver tap, and a mythical octopus,

This book is made of dreams

woven within ink.

Go ahead, reader. Open the book.

Read the narrative in verse.

You'll come empty-handed,

but leave with a gift.

Author's Note

People express their emotions in different ways. I like to think of feelings as liquid in a bottle — your mind. It has to get out somehow, whether through overflowing or by pouring it out bit by bit.

For me, poetry is the cup.

I pour my mind, my feelings into it — one poem at a time.

This collection captures the little things in life: hope, memories, imagination, and what it feels like to finally speak up after staying silent for too long.

I hope that, unlike my poem Nobody Listens, these words do more than ripple sound waves- I hope they stay with you.

— Anika

Contents

Section I — The Silence

One is silent

As they are learning to speak.

Beneath the Surface

People

like rivers:

Glimmers of lies,

Yet riptides await unseen.

Gentle currents pulling you in,

but as you sink deeper… the water darkens.

You scream.

A sudden ledge sends you

f
a
l
l
i
n
g.

At last, you understand,

Wishing you didn't.

He Does Not Know

Flaming red hair looms close.

Daggers fly from the boy's mouth.

Go back to where you came from!

Laughter rings out,

even from my friends.

My ears ache–

I sit still, silent.

He does not know

What he has said,

but *I* do.

I know

the words

weren't meant

as daggers

But instead of votes,

mere popularity.

He thinks it's cool.

Then he sees my face–

And suddenly it's not.

Outside

Outside

under the hot sun,

In the courtyard.

Laughter and gossip

fill my ears,

But my mouth

stays shut,

words stifled

by heat.

They file out—

Only I am left,

heat burning the back of my neck.

My eyes shimmering

With words I never said–

But even in the bright sun,

I stand within the shade.

Just a Seat Away

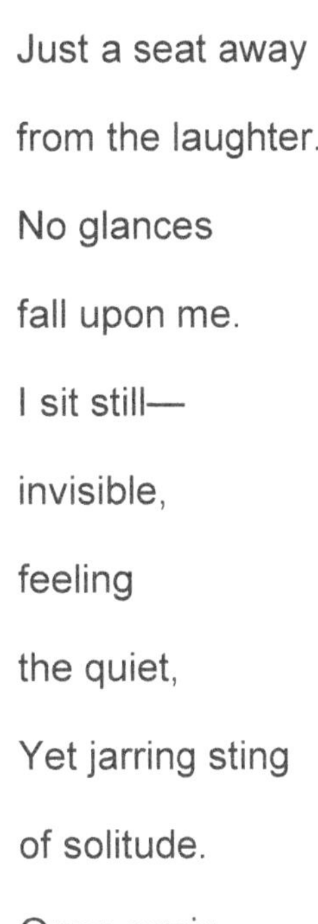

Just a seat away

from the laughter.

No glances

fall upon me.

I sit still—

invisible,

feeling

the quiet,

Yet jarring sting

of solitude.

Once again...

Nobody Listens

Mouth

opening.

Words floating out,

Feathers on the wind,

Lost in thin air.

Sound waves

Rippling.

They hear—

But they never listen.

Thin Fabric

Thin fabric

woven with thoughts

and feelings of others-

What they think of other threads,

and of me.

My hands work steadily,

trying to weave them together.

The middle stitch rips.

Surrounded by so many,
yet so lonely.

One by one,

Each stitch gives way.

I'm unraveling thread by thread

and maybe

My stitch was the only one

not in sync.

Friends

Friends —

a messy jumble of threads.

Different in many ways;

some willowy and easily bent

some tough and stubborn

some a blazing, bold red

some a smiling sunshine yellow

some a gentle humming indigo

all twined with laughter.

The same fabric,

But some are more frayed.

Still, we sew–

our knots clumsy

mending the tears

with utmost care

Our threads tangled in a way

No blade can undo.

But mine?

A lonely gray —

cast aside.

It lies alone,

thin

Yet coiled with hope

waiting

watching

hoping

to be woven in.

What If

Heart beating—

Slamming against the ribcage.

Tears rising.

What if

What if

What if

Glistening droplets

Caught upon black lashes.

What if

What if

What if...

...What if I'm not enough?

What if I never was–

And never will be?

Silence

Soft, amber lights glow.

Shadows dance across the wall.

The silence — too loud.

Section II — The Whispers

Whispers are simply

voices testing their strength.

Too Afraid

People often think

I can't find the words

to express myself.

They are wrong.

I have the perfect words—

I'm just too afraid to use them.

How could I not be?

For when I tried,

One tentative word

at a time

knowing,

Yet wanting,

carefully watching

their faces

curl to disinterest.

Gaze fell to the shoes,

words withering

within my ears.

I dreamed-

Now I don't.

Tarnished Silver Tap

Sunlight filters through trees

A faint green light rains upon me

And my smile only widens.

Tripping over roots

Little hands scraping bark

I run to the green hedge

whose leaves are somehow

always wet

And where tiny clovers sprout.

Duck behind

And I find

a tarnished silver tap.

Old and forgotten,

with a rubber yellow top,

glint reflected

in tiny white teeth.

Then I grow,

smarter and older.

My friends grow too —

taller and meaner.

They scrawl mocking words

across my hand.

The marker stings;

bright red words

insult my eyes.

When art class is over

I run, tripping over roots.

If you were ever to go

to the green hedge

whose leaves are always

somehow wet

And where tiny clovers sprout,

Duck behind and you'd find

a little girl

hair speckled with spray

thankful for her silent savior,

The tarnished silver tap.

Can't a girl just write?

Can't a girl just

Sit under a tree

By the hot summer sun

Watch the grass sway, utterly free

Like waves in the ocean.

Bright yellow pencil and paper in hand,

Scribbling away

About the feeling of warm sand.

Can't a girl just

Write whatever she'd like—

No pressure needed,

No crowd, no mic,

No stern voices

Demanding more.

...Can't a girl just write?

Hope.exe

Blorp…

System awakened

by solar energy.

Clanking

in a too-large body—

Task complete.

A human smiles at me.

Copy and paste;

I smile back.

A joke is told.

Laugh.

Error: file not found.

Humor system outdated.

Initiate protocol;

Nod and shuffle

back to charging port.

Shut down.

Maybe—

hopefully—

an update

will be available

The next morning.

Section III — The Voice Within

A voice is richest

the minute before it speaks.

Tainted Red

The octopus —

It wasn't always inky black.

Used to be a boring gray,

something plain, something nobody

looked twice at.

So it stole others' books,

and covered itself in the ink.

Inky black shadow,

 tentacles desperate,

flailing in every direction,

reaching out for

a hue of its own.

But then the octopus looks down,

sees color beneath the black.

Wipes off the ink and finds-

Red? Not gray.

It realizes-

Color bloomed when it wasn't looking.

Finally, it has something to call

its own.

Tentacles scramble

to wipe away black ink,

But ink leaves a stain.

The octopus cries

salty tears.

Its red shall be

forever tainted.

The Desk, the Closet, and the Shadow

Crickets chirp softly

as moonlight filters through shades.

Shadows drape

half the room.

A tree's branch

sways gently

out the window.

Lost within visions

of crazy dreams,

a wry smile on your face.

GRR.

cuts through the quiet.

Eyes fly open,

pupils dilated.

GRR.

A warning?

Breath quickens,

head whipping

side to side.

GRR.

Springs groan

As you sit up,

leaves' shadow

curling

ominously.

GRR.

Is it getting closer?

Is it even real?

GRR.

The closet?

Behind the desk?

Within the shadow?

Next to you?

GRR.

Heart stops.

You turn

ever so gently,

carefully,

quietly—

and see—

GRR.

Your brother's

been snoring

the whole time.

GRR.

Imagination–

too vivid can be

Such a curse.

Reality

Don't brains feel like clouds?

sometimes light and weightless,

Sometimes holding storms?

Seemingly fluffy and soft,

a great place to lie down

and relax.

A place that can hold me.

But in reality,

made of cold air

that I fall through,

shivering all the while.

Never Ending

Drip. Drip. Drip.

Down the window,

my fingers chase

gleaming droplets

that slides down the glass.

Skin touches cold water,

and pulls back

sharply.

The droplet keeps sliding, Unfazed.

Brown eyes stare,

Ears listening

to the constant

drip drop

of the rain.

Worries, I can't stop—

again,

again,

again.

Never-ending.

Overflow

Wells.

Water sometimes overflows.

You build them higher

But soon enough—

WHOOSH.

Stone cracks.

Water floods.

Yet you watch

gaze avoiding the water's surface

for when they touch–

You'll see your reflection

distorted

eyes rippling

with guilt

Others should have felt

But you carried it in a bucket,

rusted and groaning,

and dumped the water

down a well.

Shatter

FWOOSH.

Freezing water

dumped into

fragile glass.

Liquid swirling

With icy anger—

The glass seems to tremble.

I remain silent

watching

waiting

knowing

Hearing the glass shatter

before it ever does.

But then…

KRISSSSSSH!

I duck for cover—

and later

Only I remain…

Silently sweeping the shards.

But then…

Breath fogs the scene.

Head whirling

I realize…

I've been looking

not at glass but

a mirror

The entire time.

And in the pieces

My own eyes stare back-

the fragments

glittering sadly

With knowing.

Whirling

Whirling winds shriek

Lightning slashes through the sky

Yet I stand steady.

Hatred

Hatred…

Oh, how it works like wine!

Strong, bold-flavored.

Yet if you keep it in too long,

It turns to vinegar.

A bitter trace,

nothing but a fine powder.

But still it remains—

Waiting to be let out of the bottle.

My Creatures

Creatures

that spring forth

from my dreams.

THUD.

THUD.

THUD.

Banging against

the rough edges of my mind.

Tumbling,

Whirling,

Twisting,

Fighting to come out.

Yet I hold them fast,

knowing the pain

they'd bring

if others saw them.

The sharp, biting daggers

that would fly from mouths.

No—never.

I must hold them fast

No matter how much

I long to let go.

A battering ram charges—

SMASH.
CRASH.
SLASH.

Walls falling, exposing me—

My creatures

revealed.

I no longer need to hide.

But just as I feared—

glances sharp enough

to cut through

What daggers cannot.

But maybe I don't care.

For in the light,

My creatures glow

Not shyly,

Not bravely,

But real—

The only realness

In the room.

And suddenly, I know—

They were too beautiful

to hide away for long.

For the world needs them

And so do I.

Section IV — Finally Spoken

You won't always be heard.

But it's enough if those who do hear

truly listen.

After the Storm

Sun rays peek through the clouds.

Like a balloon, filled with hope.

Soft petals emerge.

Remnants

Dewdrops upon a leaf

Quiet echoes of a memory

Curl my lips upward

Looking for Another Smile

A bundle of fluff…

gray and white,

lies at my feet.

I pet the bunny,

feeling its cotton fur.

Lips curl up,

quiet tears of joy.

I glance around,

looking for another smile.

Emptiness.

But then I realize—

Why look for another smile

when mine is enough?

Scars

Blades

Once pierced my skin.

The scars remain—

But blades dull over time.

Cuts mend themselves.

And life goes on—

The mark remains,

but the hatred?

forever gone.

As I Prepare to Speak

Deep breaths

in and out

as I walk into the room.

At last,

every eye finds me

as I prepare to speak.

And at last-

My eyes

find theirs.

My creatures

were revealed.

Now

they are shown.

Glass Walls

Hiding behind fogged glass walls,

I think they can't see me.

Their eyes drift past the fog,

never seeing

That I'm afraid,

that I'm lonely,

that I'm quiet,

And they don't ask.

I scream it all,

The echoes bouncing back to me.

My voice trapped

In the glass walls I built.

But they hear.

They turn.

And so do I.

Fog clears

eyes meet

two hands on glass—

not touching,

But almost.

Gaze filled with pain

and something like

wonder.

Breath frosts the now-clear glass

It's fog once hiding

Both our pain.

I never knew.

Now you do.

Twin smiles,

sad

but now shared.

Bright Blue Broom

Upon the dusty kitchen floor,

checkered tiles covered

by fragments of thread,

shards of glass,

rivulets of water,

and spilt vinegar—

Sits a girl, cross-legged.

Her eyes stare ahead,

unseeing, unfocused,

unsure where to begin.

Thud.

Thud.

Footsteps?

The girl rises,

black hair rippling.

She faces the woman,

And her lips slowly part.

Fingers reaching out,

brushing a woman's skin,

like thoughts twirling between

What's a dream and what's not?

The woman,

a perfect reflection,

as if she were *the girl* –

but older, calmer,

motions to the girl's feet.

Brows twisting,

brown eyes look at the cluttered floor.

In the midst of the dust lies:

a broom,

bright blue,

With a dustpan beside.

It's yours.

And with that, the woman leaves,

The girl's eyes following

intricate wicker sandals.

Her breath stills.

Arms reaching down–

palms quaking

fingers closing

upon a bright blue broom.

Hands finger straw bristles;

how rough, how thin.

Yet how necessary…

Her breath now steady,

dustpan clutched within the left hand,

The girl sweeps

dust and questions swirling.

Maybe the woman brought the broom.

Or maybe it was behind her all along…

like yours is.

Just waiting

to be picked up.

She finishes now

dustpan tucked away

With tender hands

that know

She may need it again.

And once more,

The girl gazes at her kitchen.

Lips curl up.

No clutter in sight

It's finally clear

finally free—

to create.

The girl glances over her shoulder

brown eyes catching the woman's shadow.

A smile plays on the girl's lips.

Now it's time to cook.

CLICK

The camera

lies alone and soaked

on the soggy wooden porch

after the storm.

Everyone gathers—

Oh no, it's ruined!

Sighs of regret.

But suddenly—

CLICK!

A flash of bright white.

All eyes rest upon

the newly taken picture.

Mouths open—

they realize:

The rain never

ruined the camera,

Just washed its lens

so it could see in greater detail.

But maybe the vividness

could be what ruins it—

For the world can be

an ugly sight to see.

Or maybe the vividness
It is what brings hope,
for pictures carry
smiles that last for decades.

I suppose it's all up to
what the camera chooses
to take a picture of.

For You

Words whistling impatiently,

pressing at the edge—

like a kettle on the stove,

steam building beneath the lid.

The tower grows too tall—

And the stone cracks.

Now they come pouring out,

perfect words

chosen long ago.

Like threads, frayed

all different colors and textures.

Some spiral,

whirling,

wondering what if.

Some simply show

What it's like

for dreams

to fly out of your head.

Some are memories—

silent

Yet true.

And some?

Some are being told

this very moment—

to you.

Harmony

Distant stars glimmer,

Owls hoot, crickets chirp, wolves howl

Not many— but one.

The Choice

A strange, curved seed

buried beneath sand.

High tide

comes and goes

and the seed?

It sprouts-

not bright, leafy kelp

But an inky black creature

with tentacles that curl

In a way, both beautiful

and venomous.

Never meant to grow

But it doesn't care.

The octopus rises,

And from its appendages drips—

ink that spreads in the water

transforming into murky words.

Some float to the surface,

glistening in the sun,

desperate to be seen.

Others settle in the sand

with soft sighs of relief.

The rest dance around you,

bobbing gently in the waves.

Octopus turns to face you-

violet gaze pierces yours.

An unspoken question…

Will you accept the gift?

The words?

Or will you leave them

lost within the blue?

About the Author

Anika Yadav is a young poet with an observant mind and a heart attuned to metaphor. At twelve years old, she draws inspiration from everyday moments—watching, listening, and shaping silence into stanzas that speak.

Born in India and now living in Texas, Anika explores a wide range of themes in her writing, from quiet emotion to thoughtful philosophy. Her debut poetry collection invites readers to recognize themselves-past or present-in every line.

When she's not writing, Anika loves getting lost in novels, dancing, and encouraging other young voices to share their stories.

"Every voice has value; it just needs to make the world see it."